THE
LAST
CYCLOPS

written and illustrated by
Sarah Goodnow Riley-Land

THE LAST CYCLOPS

This book was a labor of love -
THANK YOU for not copying it or distributing it
in nefarious ways.

If you'd like to use the text or images from THE LAST CYCLOPS
please contact the author.

This is a work of fiction. Any similarity between the characters
and situations within its pages and places or persons, living
or dead, is unintentional and co-incidental.
Except for the cyclops. That part is real.

To my home state of Missouri

The people of the long canoe
may be long gone
but their namesake river pulses still

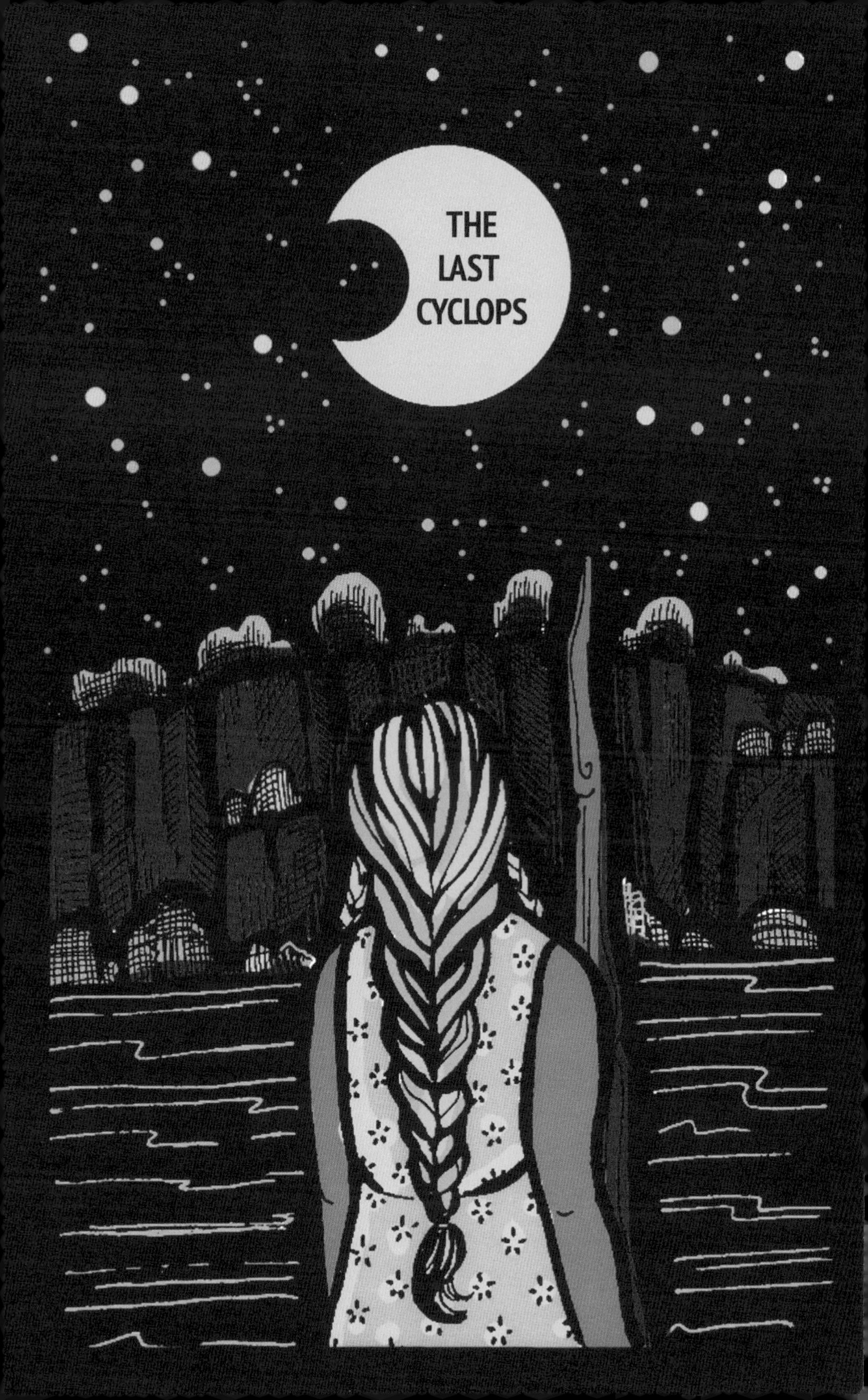
THE
LAST
CYCLOPS

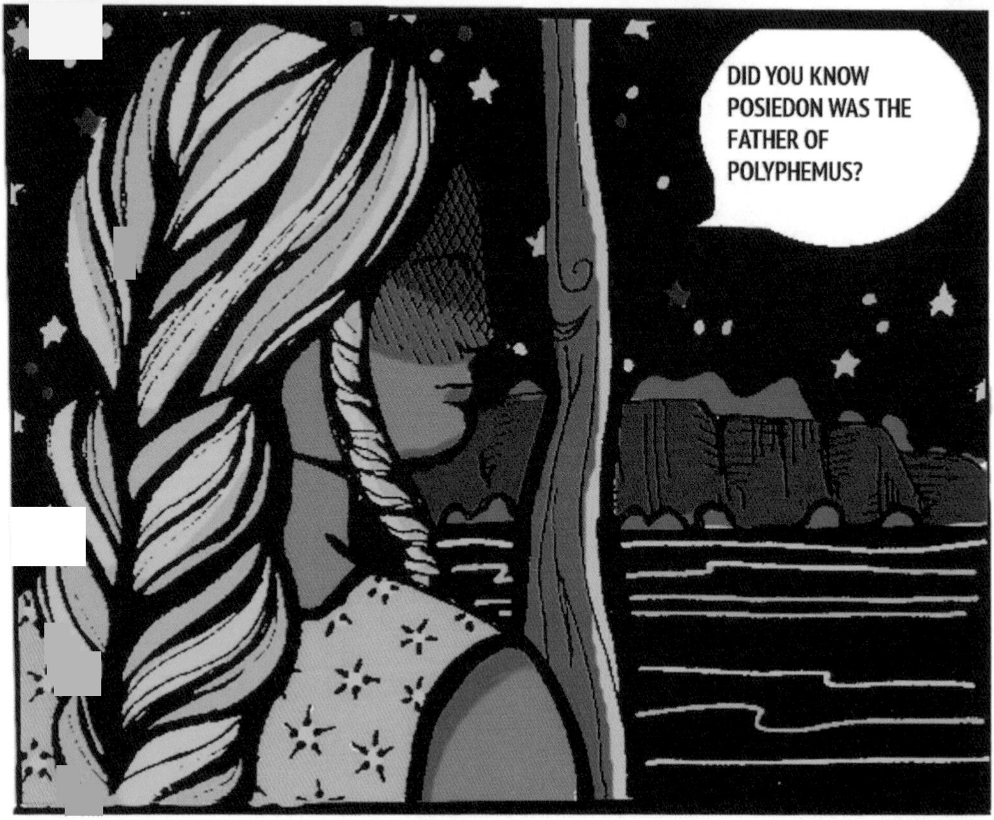
DID YOU KNOW POSIEDON WAS THE FATHER OF POLYPHEMUS?

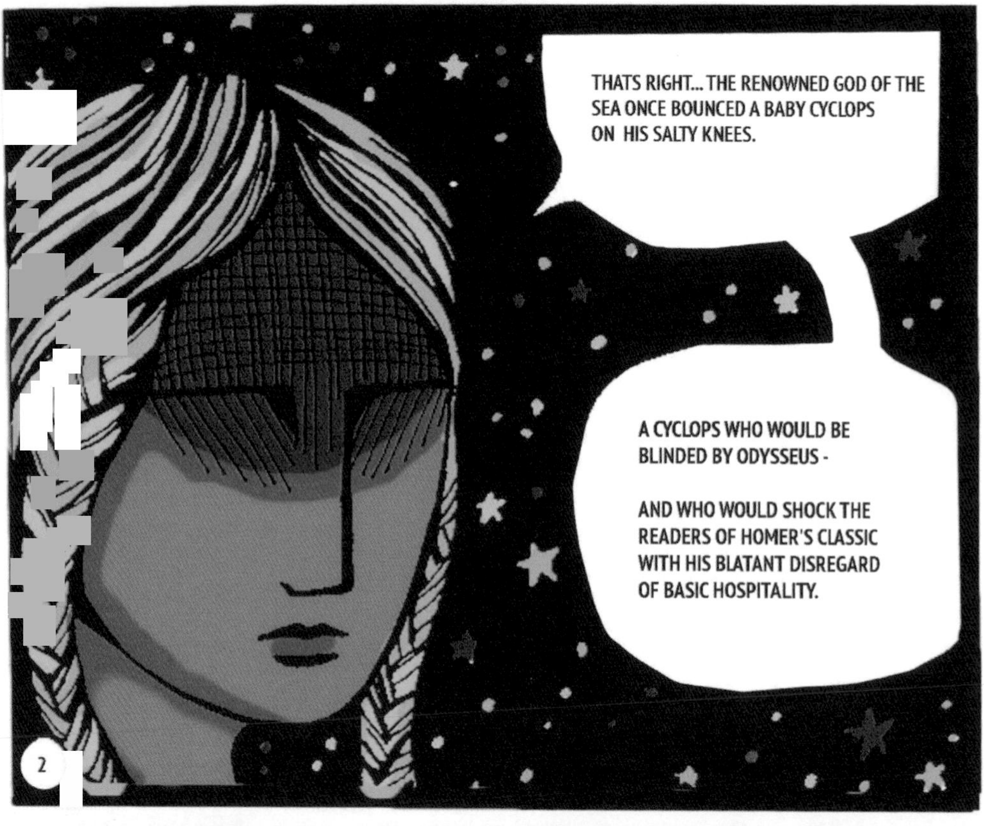
THATS RIGHT... THE RENOWNED GOD OF THE SEA ONCE BOUNCED A BABY CYCLOPS ON HIS SALTY KNEES.
A CYCLOPS WHO WOULD BE BLINDED BY ODYSSEUS -
AND WHO WOULD SHOCK THE READERS OF HOMER'S CLASSIC WITH HIS BLATANT DISREGARD OF BASIC HOSPITALITY.

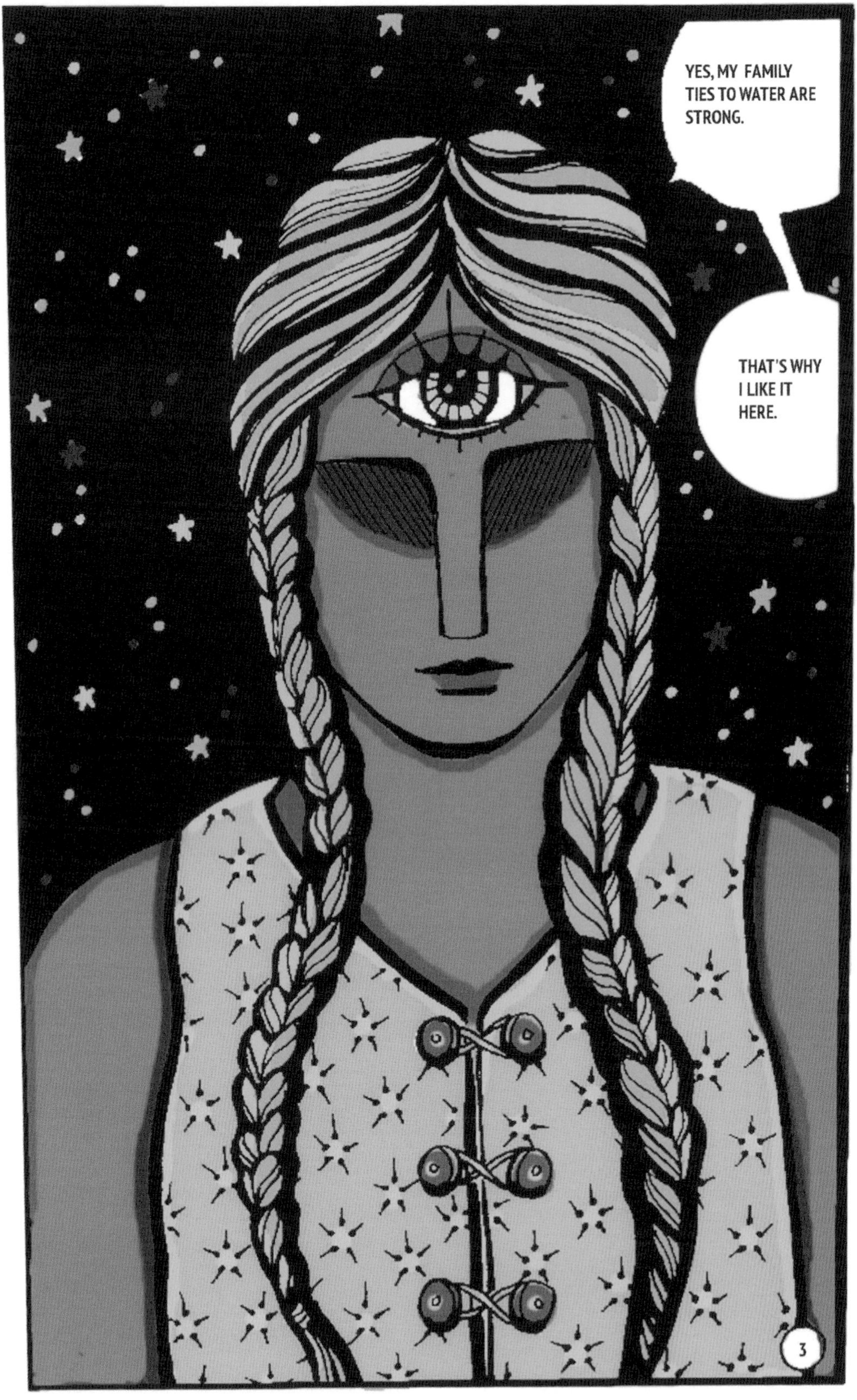
YES, MY FAMILY TIES TO WATER ARE STRONG.
THAT'S WHY I LIKE IT HERE.

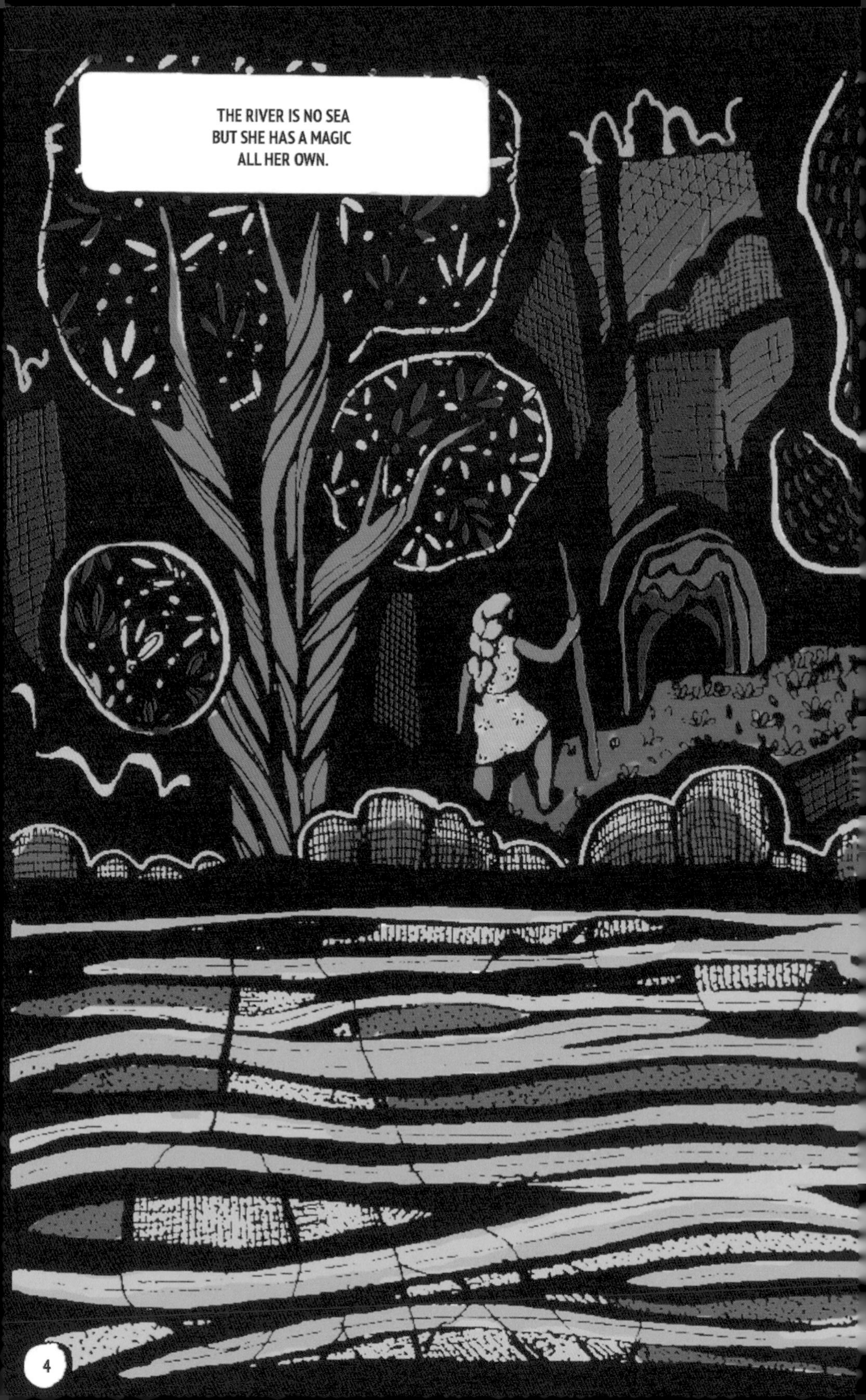
THE RIVER IS NO SEA
BUT SHE HAS A MAGIC
ALL HER OWN.

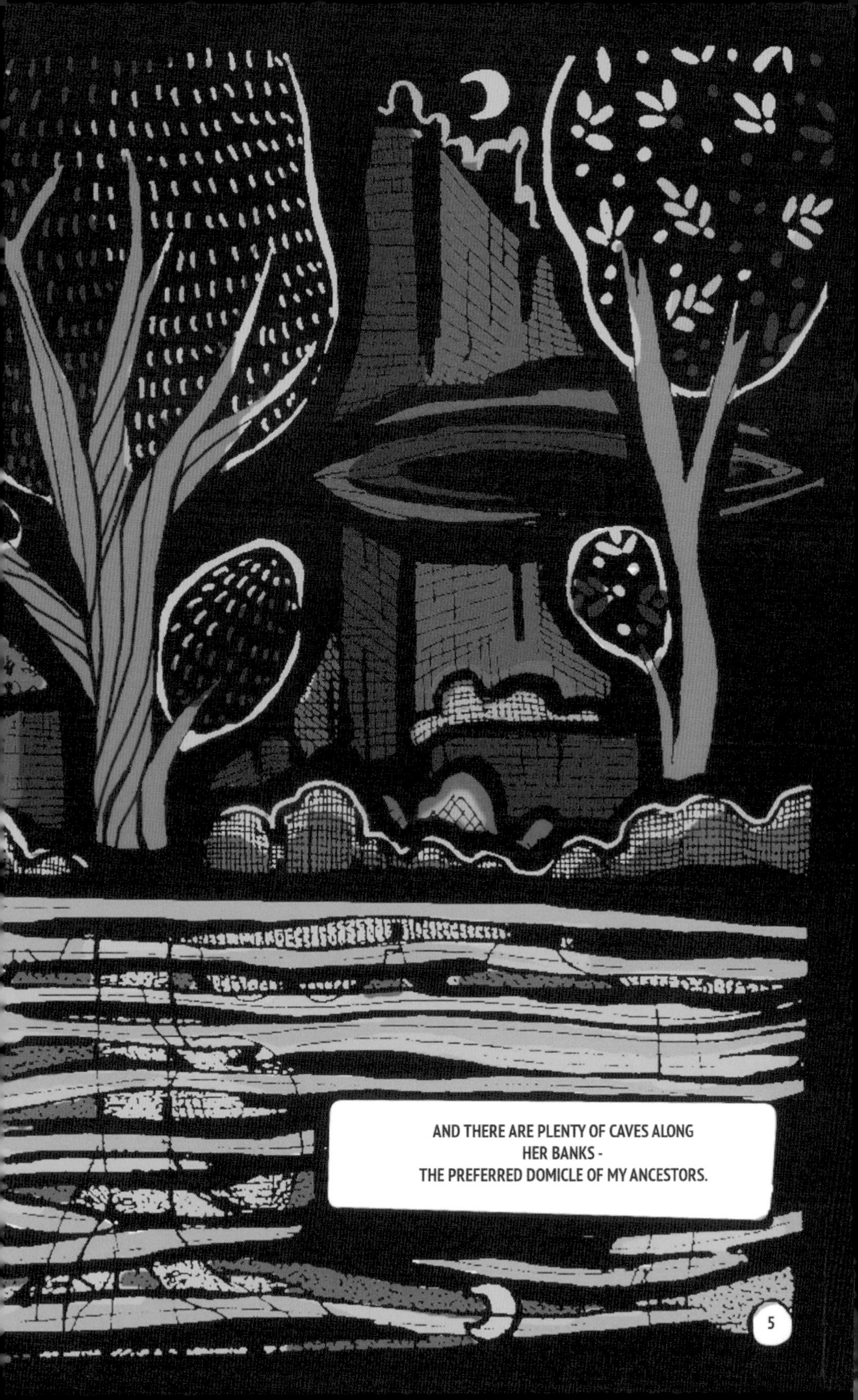
AND THERE ARE PLENTY OF CAVES ALONG
HER BANKS -
THE PREFERRED DOMICLE OF MY ANCESTORS.

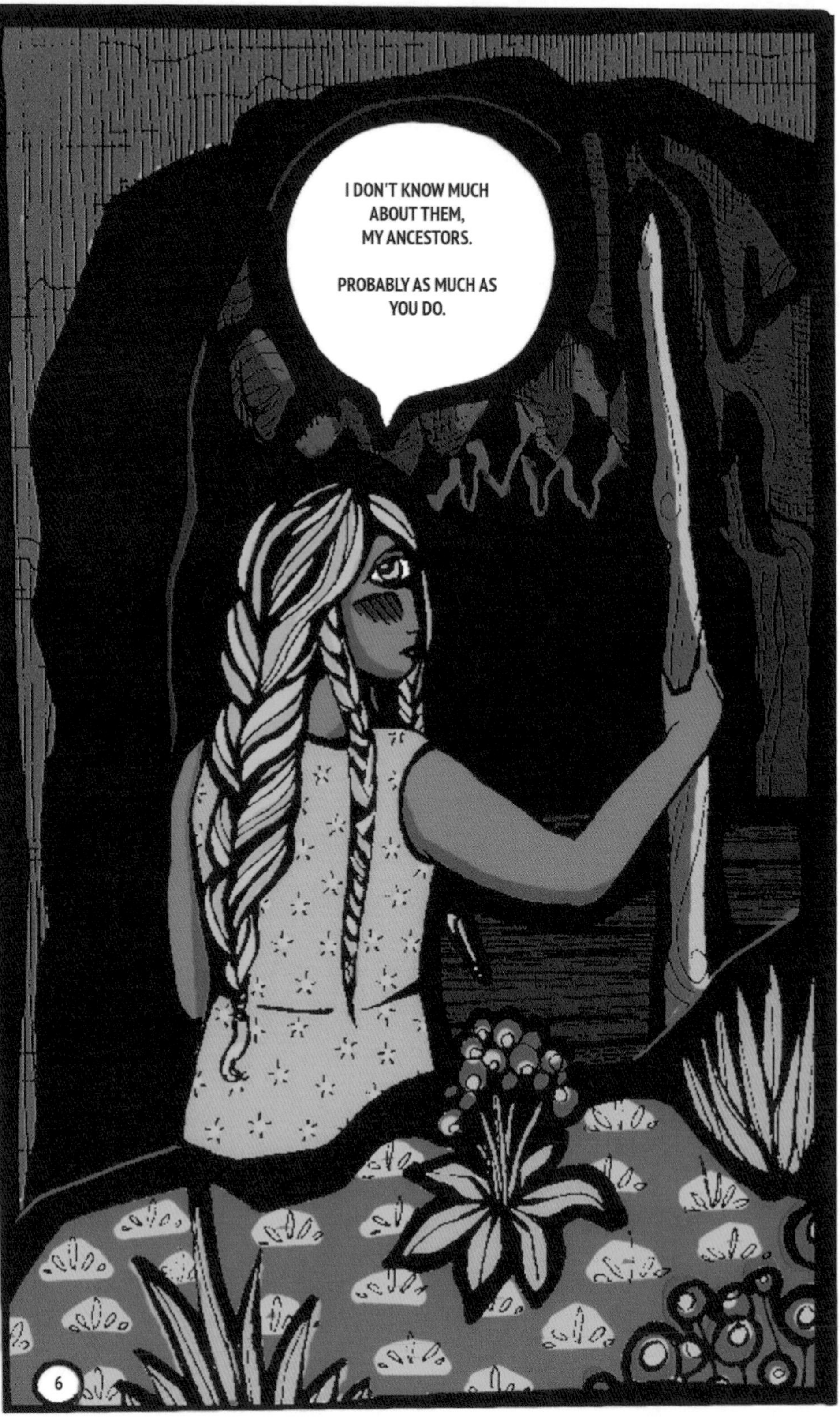
I DON'T KNOW MUCH ABOUT THEM, MY ANCESTORS.
PROBABLY AS MUCH AS YOU DO.

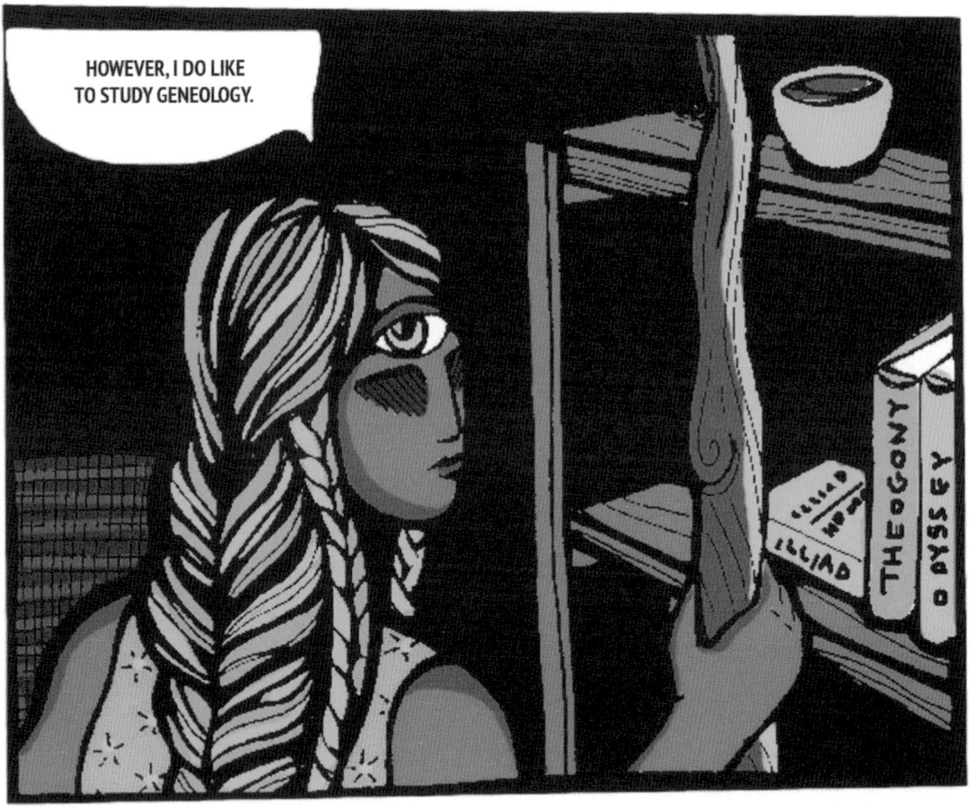
HOWEVER, I DO LIKE
TO STUDY GENEOLOGY.
ILLIAD
THEOGONY
ODYSSEY

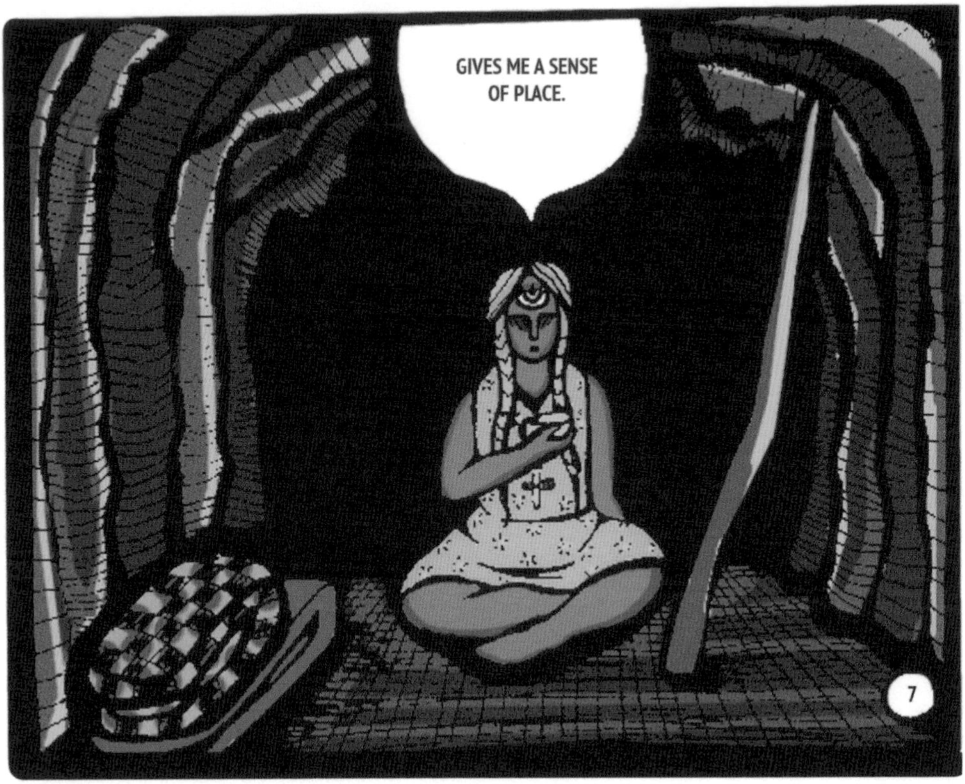
GIVES ME A SENSE
OF PLACE.

POLYPHEMUS IS MY GRANDFATHER THOUGH I'VE NEVER MET THE FELLOW.
IF HE'S STILL AROUND, I RECKON HE'S IN THE OLD COUNTRY.
A LONG TIME AGO MY PARENTS AND SOME NYMPHS AND THE LIKE, NO ONE YOU WOULD KNOW, MADE THE MOVE TO THIS PART OF THE WORLD.

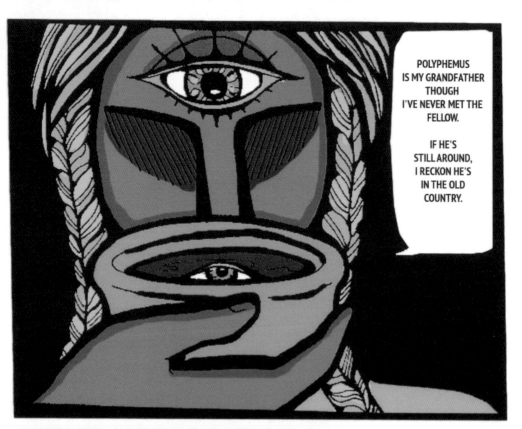

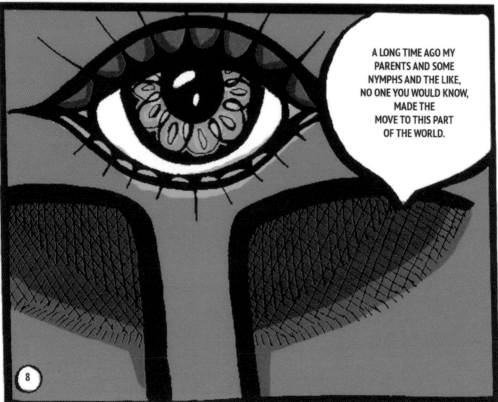

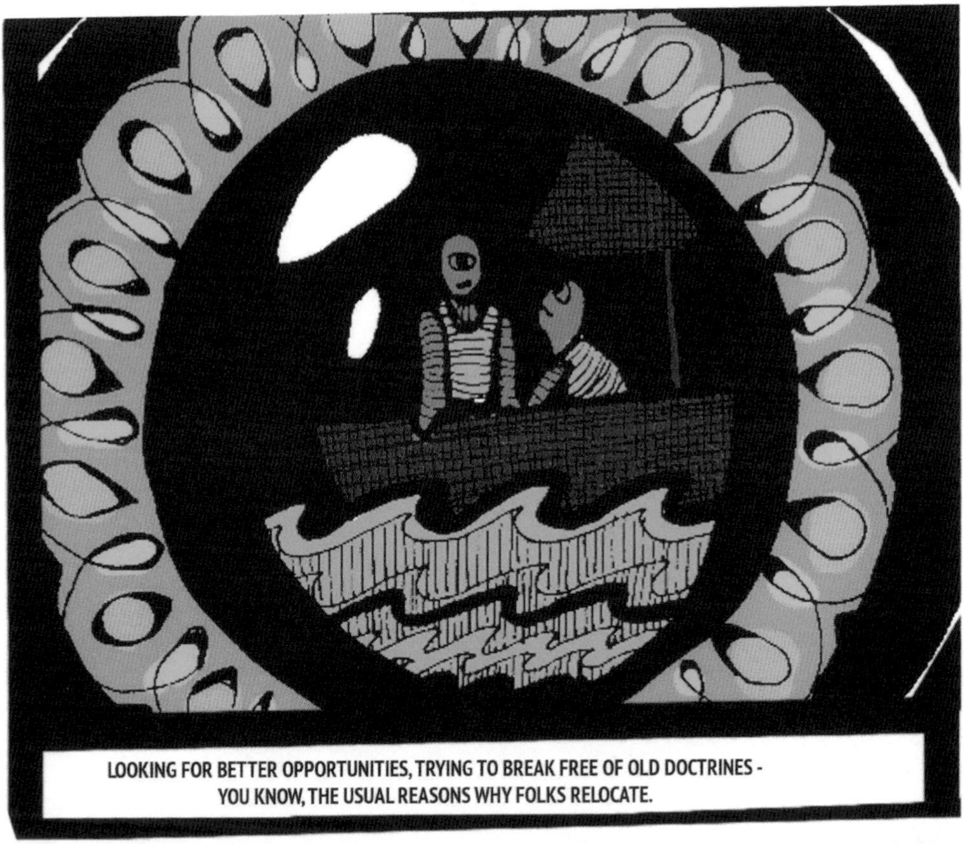
LOOKING FOR BETTER OPPORTUNITIES, TRYING TO BREAK FREE OF OLD DOCTRINES - YOU KNOW, THE USUAL REASONS WHY FOLKS RELOCATE.

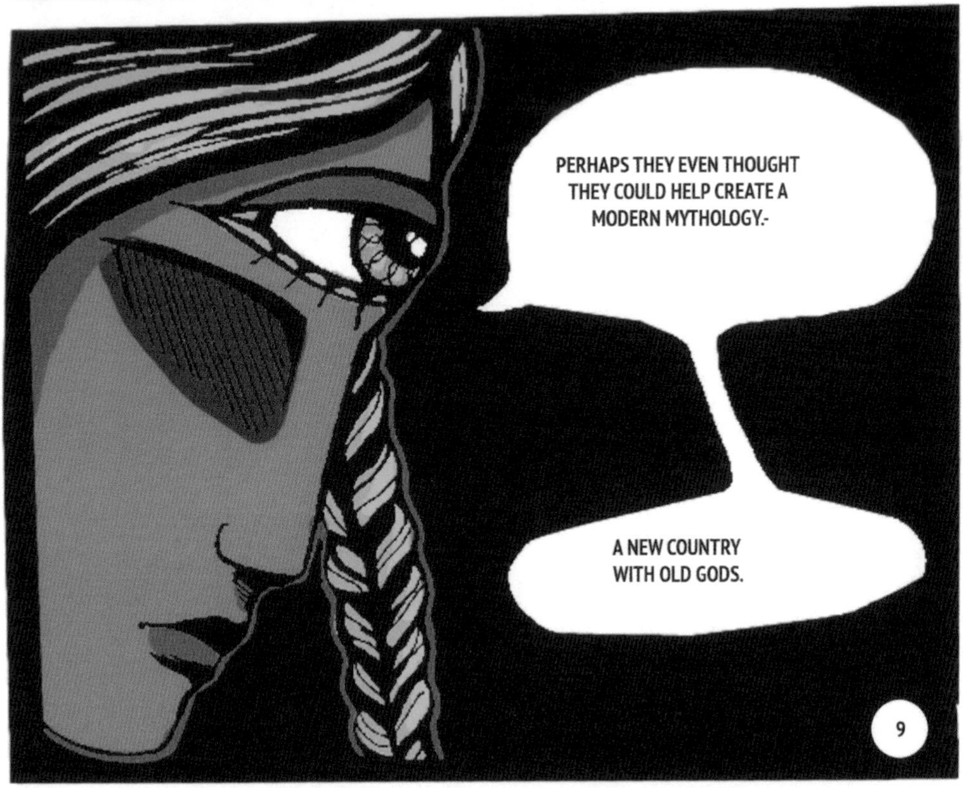
PERHAPS THEY EVEN THOUGHT THEY COULD HELP CREATE A MODERN MYTHOLOGY.-
A NEW COUNTRY WITH OLD GODS.

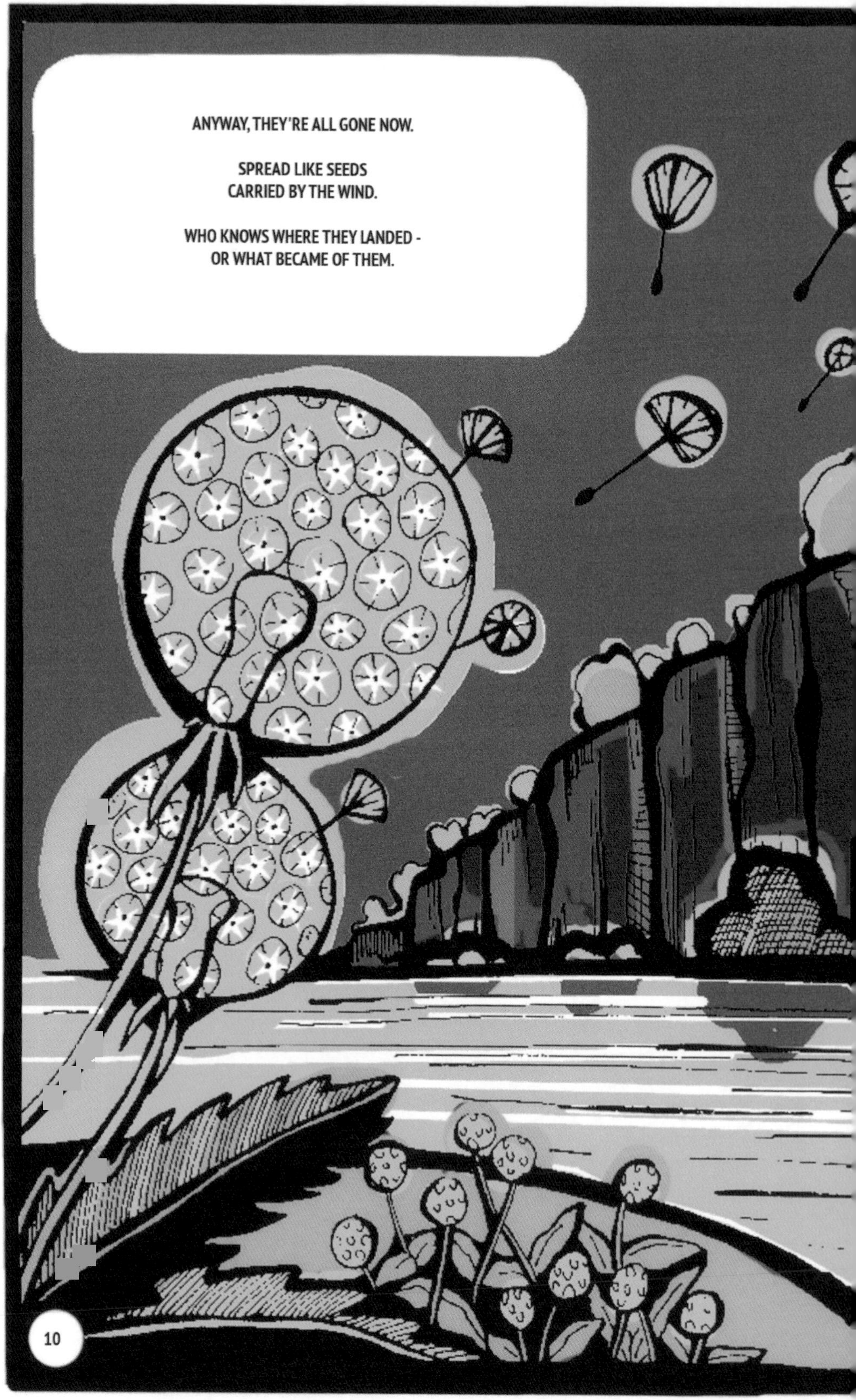
ANYWAY, THEY'RE ALL GONE NOW.
SPREAD LIKE SEEDS
CARRIED BY THE WIND.
WHO KNOWS WHERE THEY LANDED -
OR WHAT BECAME OF THEM.

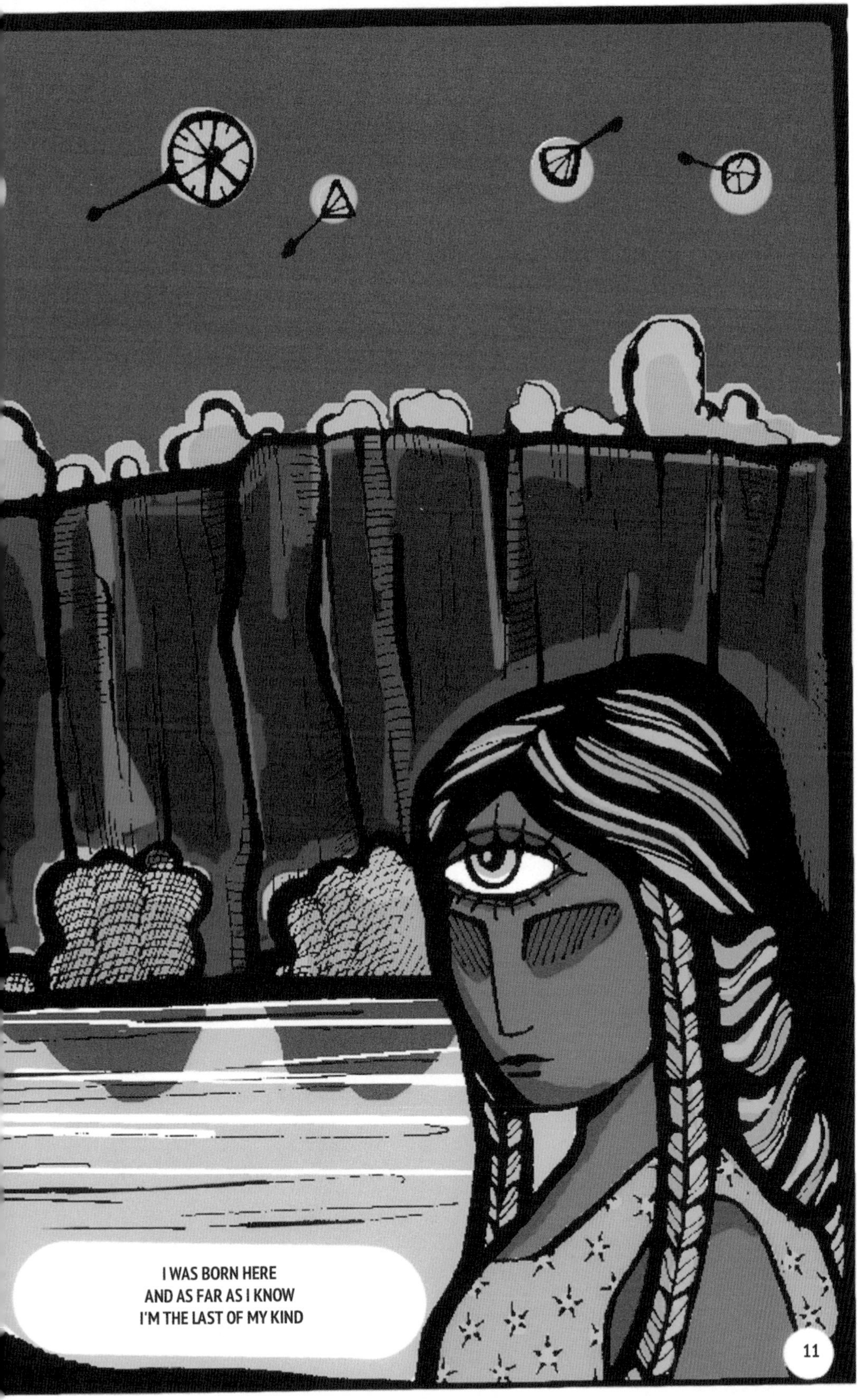
I WAS BORN HERE
AND AS FAR AS I KNOW
I'M THE LAST OF MY KIND

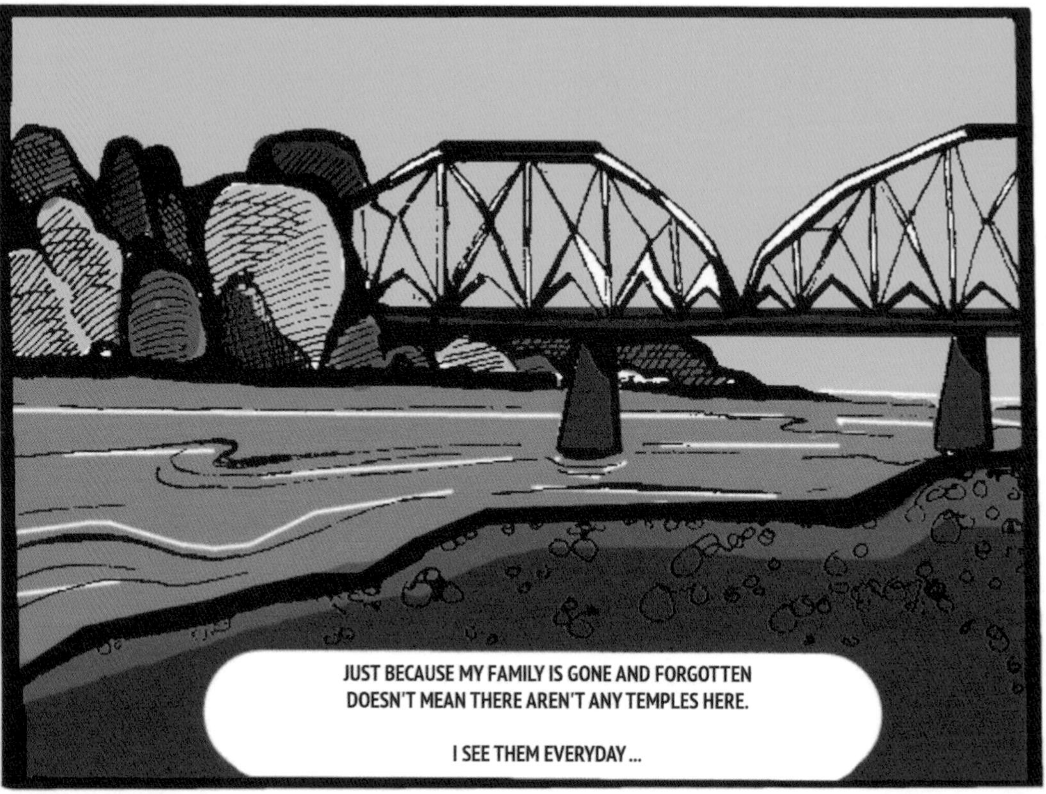
JUST BECAUSE MY FAMILY IS GONE AND FORGOTTEN DOESN'T MEAN THERE AREN'T ANY TEMPLES HERE.
I SEE THEM EVERYDAY...

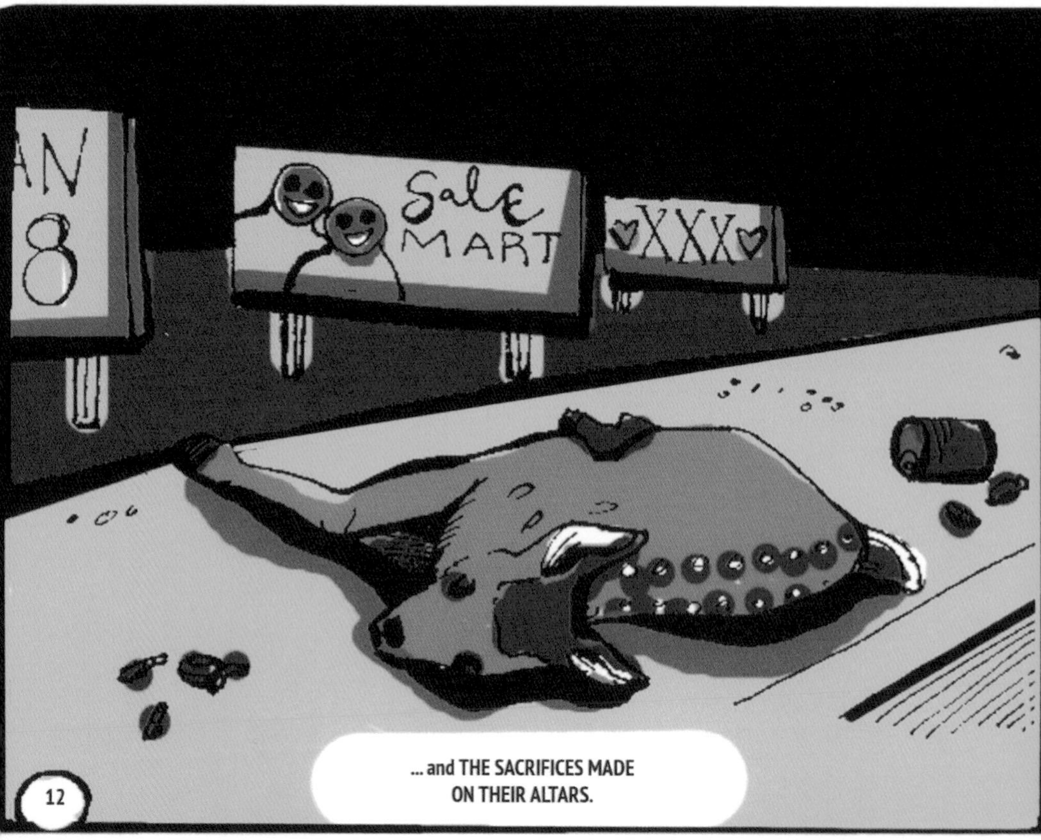
Sale MART
XXX
... and THE SACRIFICES MADE ON THEIR ALTARS.

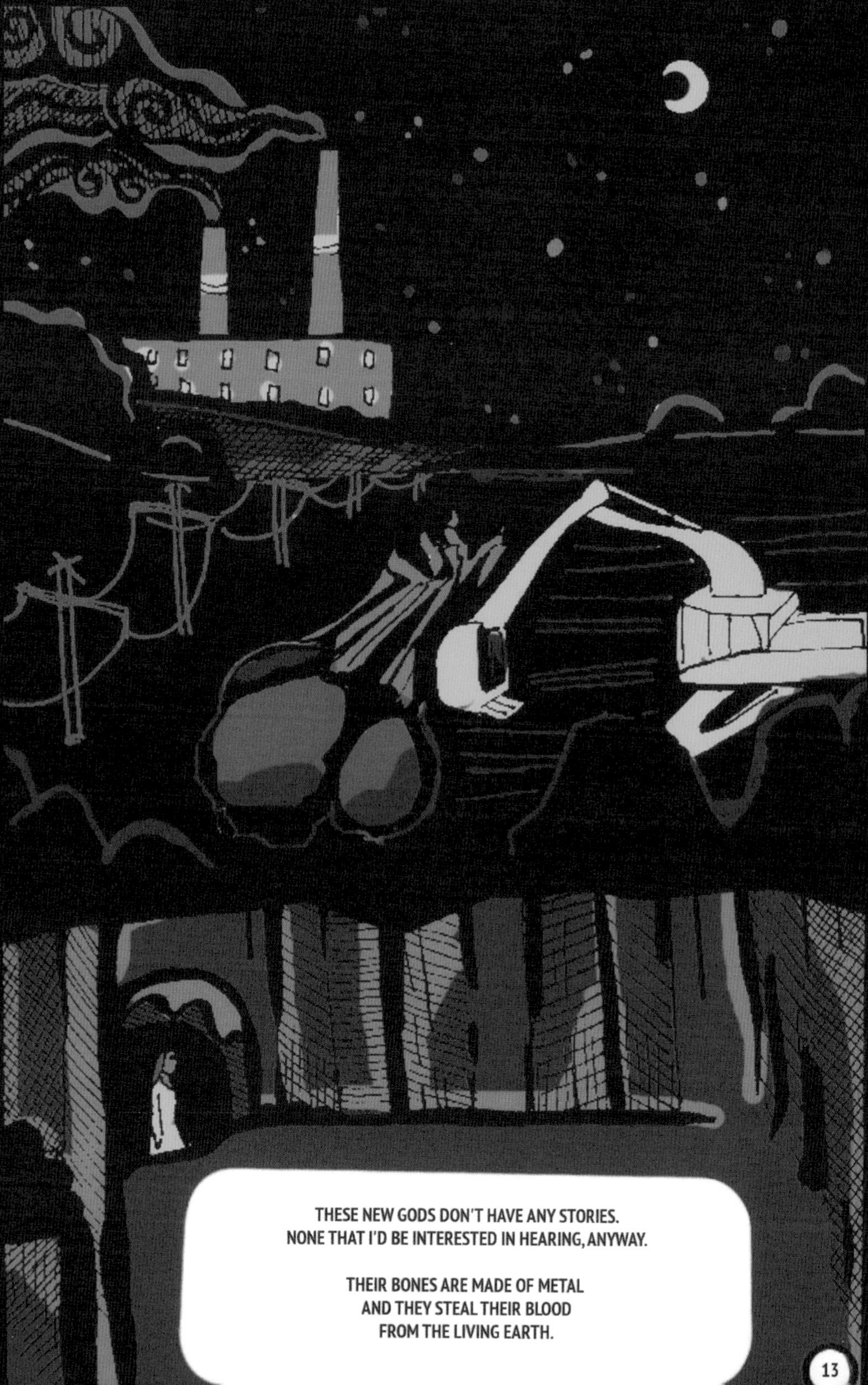
THESE NEW GODS DON'T HAVE ANY STORIES.
NONE THAT I'D BE INTERESTED IN HEARING, ANYWAY.
THEIR BONES ARE MADE OF METAL
AND THEY STEAL THEIR BLOOD
FROM THE LIVING EARTH.

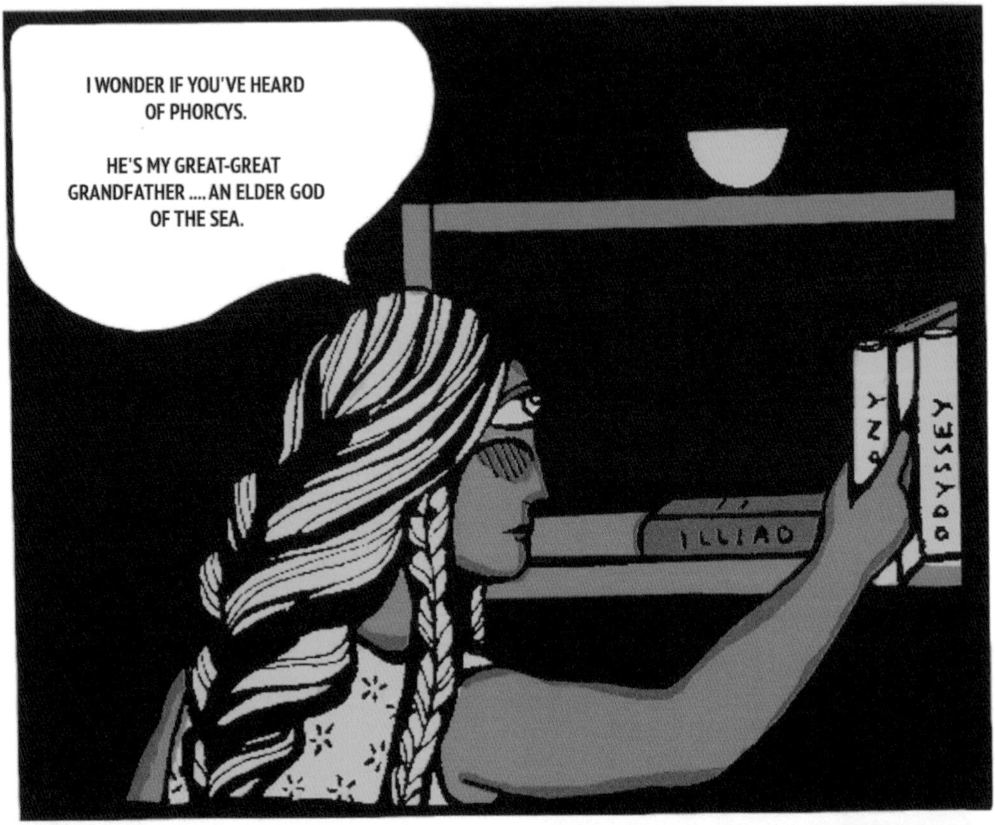
I WONDER IF YOU'VE HEARD OF PHORCYS.
HE'S MY GREAT-GREAT GRANDFATHER .... AN ELDER GOD OF THE SEA.
ODYSSEY
ILLIAD

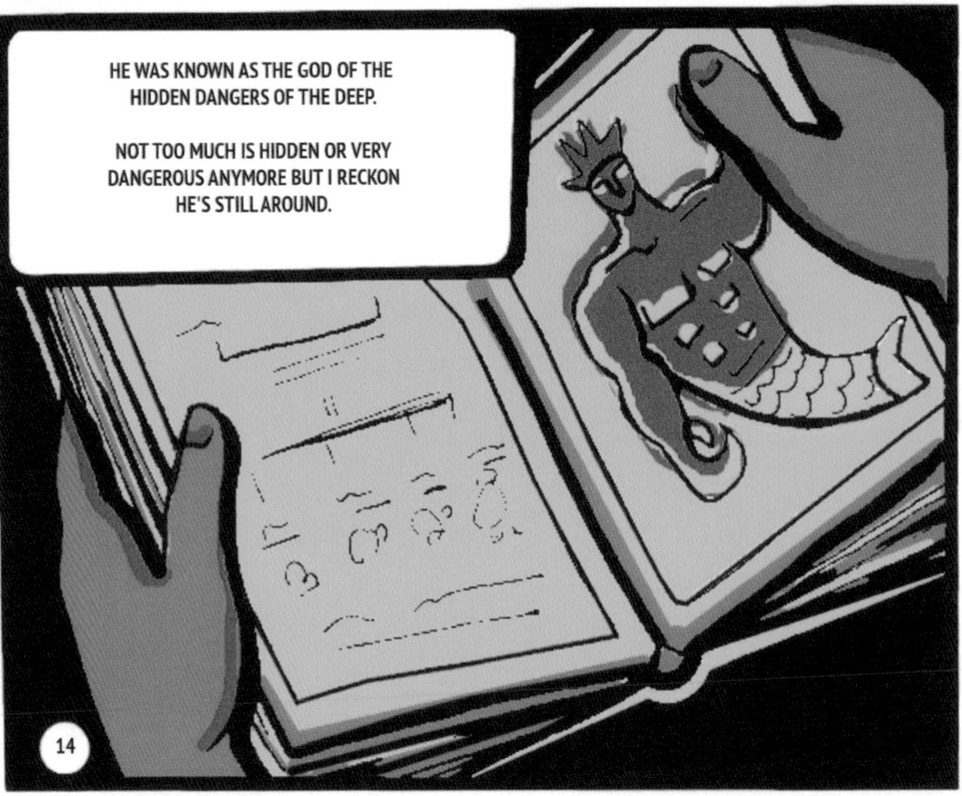
HE WAS KNOWN AS THE GOD OF THE HIDDEN DANGERS OF THE DEEP.
NOT TOO MUCH IS HIDDEN OR VERY DANGEROUS ANYMORE BUT I RECKON HE'S STILL AROUND.

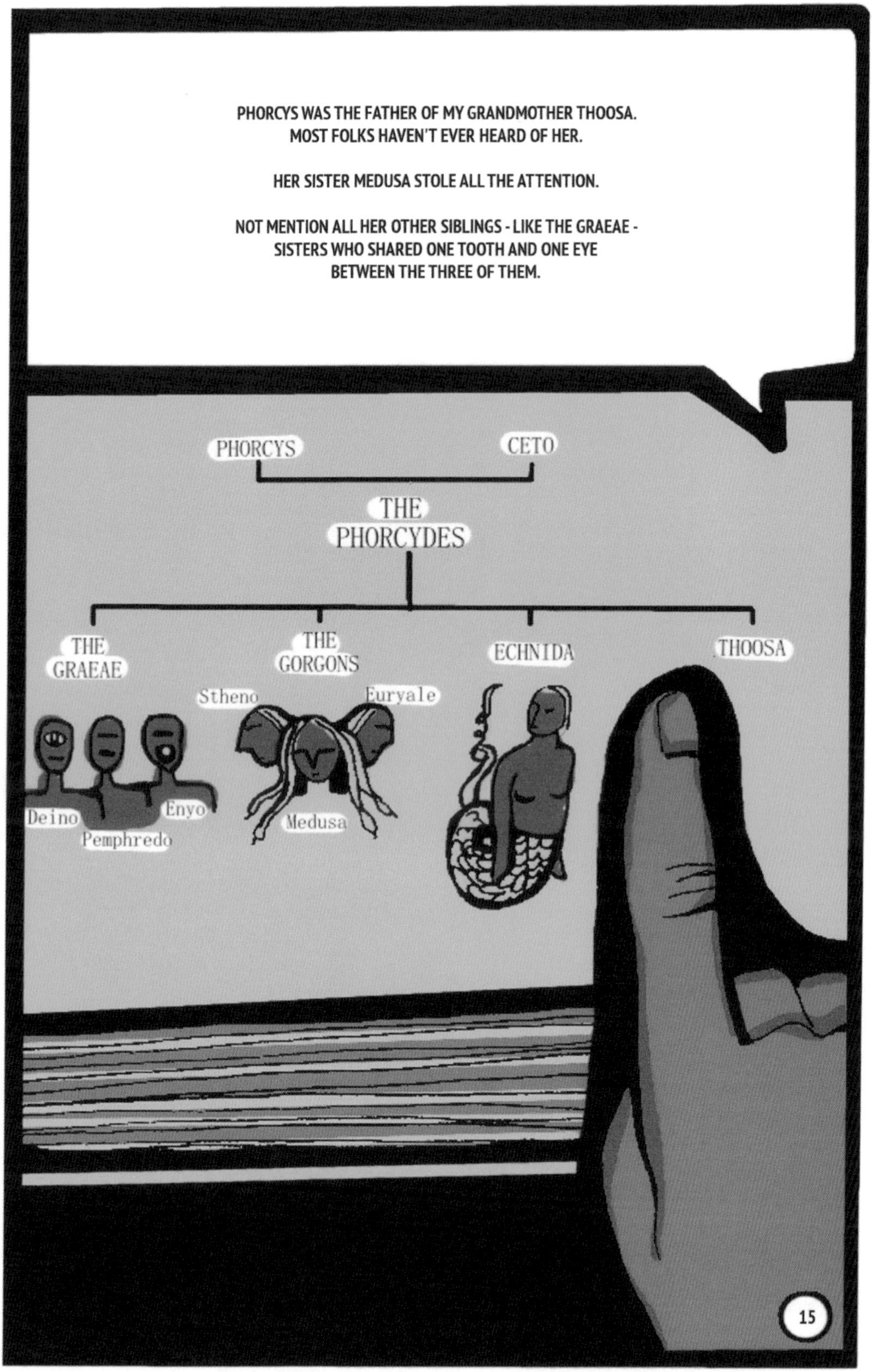
PHORCYS WAS THE FATHER OF MY GRANDMOTHER THOOSA.
MOST FOLKS HAVEN'T EVER HEARD OF HER.
HER SISTER MEDUSA STOLE ALL THE ATTENTION.
NOT MENTION ALL HER OTHER SIBLINGS - LIKE THE GRAEAE - SISTERS WHO SHARED ONE TOOTH AND ONE EYE BETWEEN THE THREE OF THEM.
PHORCYS
CETO
THE PHORCYDES
THE GRAEAE
THE GORGONS
ECHNIDA
THOOSA
Stheno
Euryale
Deino
Pemphredo
Enyo
Medusa

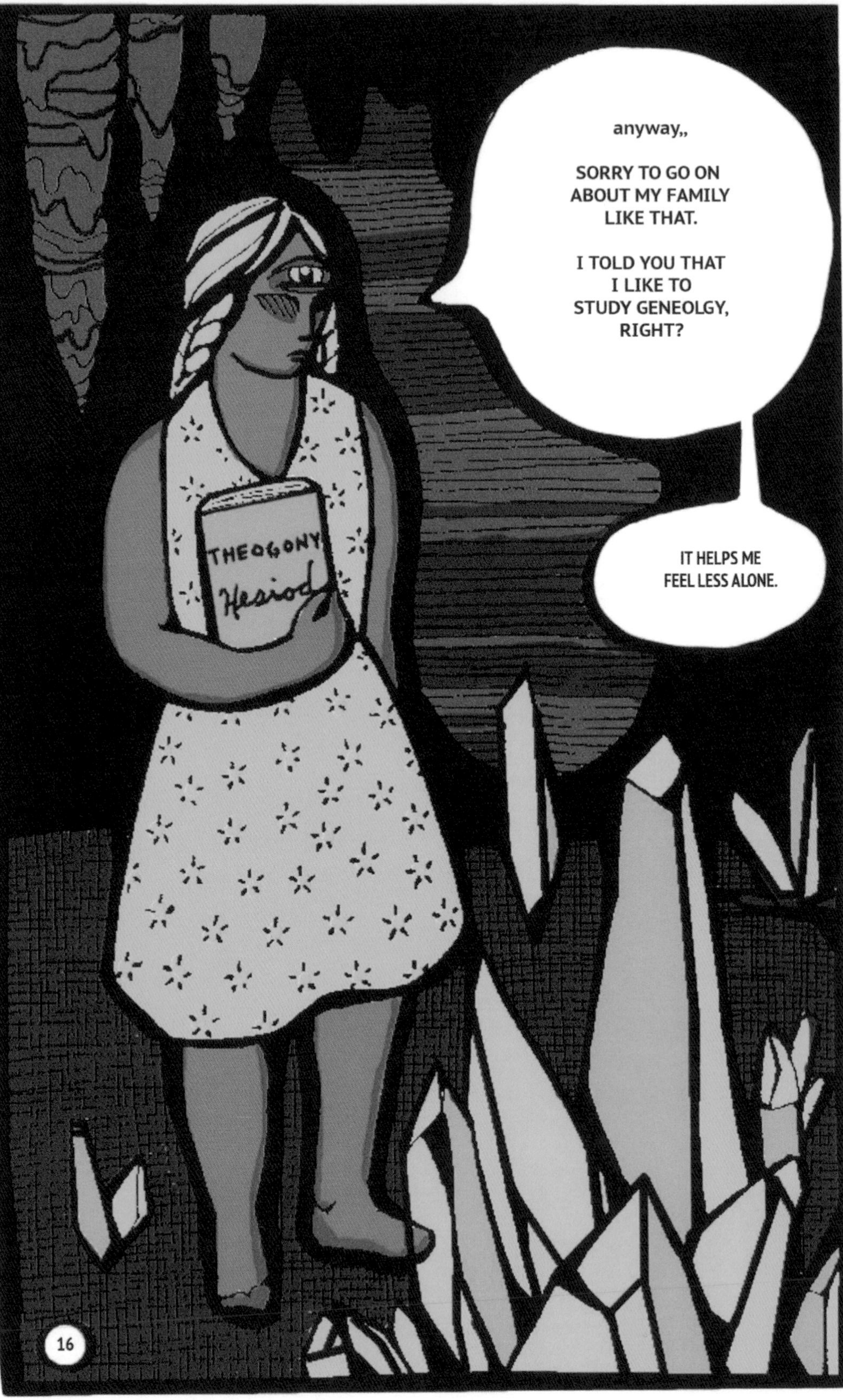
anyway,,
SORRY TO GO ON ABOUT MY FAMILY LIKE THAT.
I TOLD YOU THAT I LIKE TO STUDY GENEOLGY, RIGHT?
IT HELPS ME FEEL LESS ALONE.
THEOGONY Hesiod

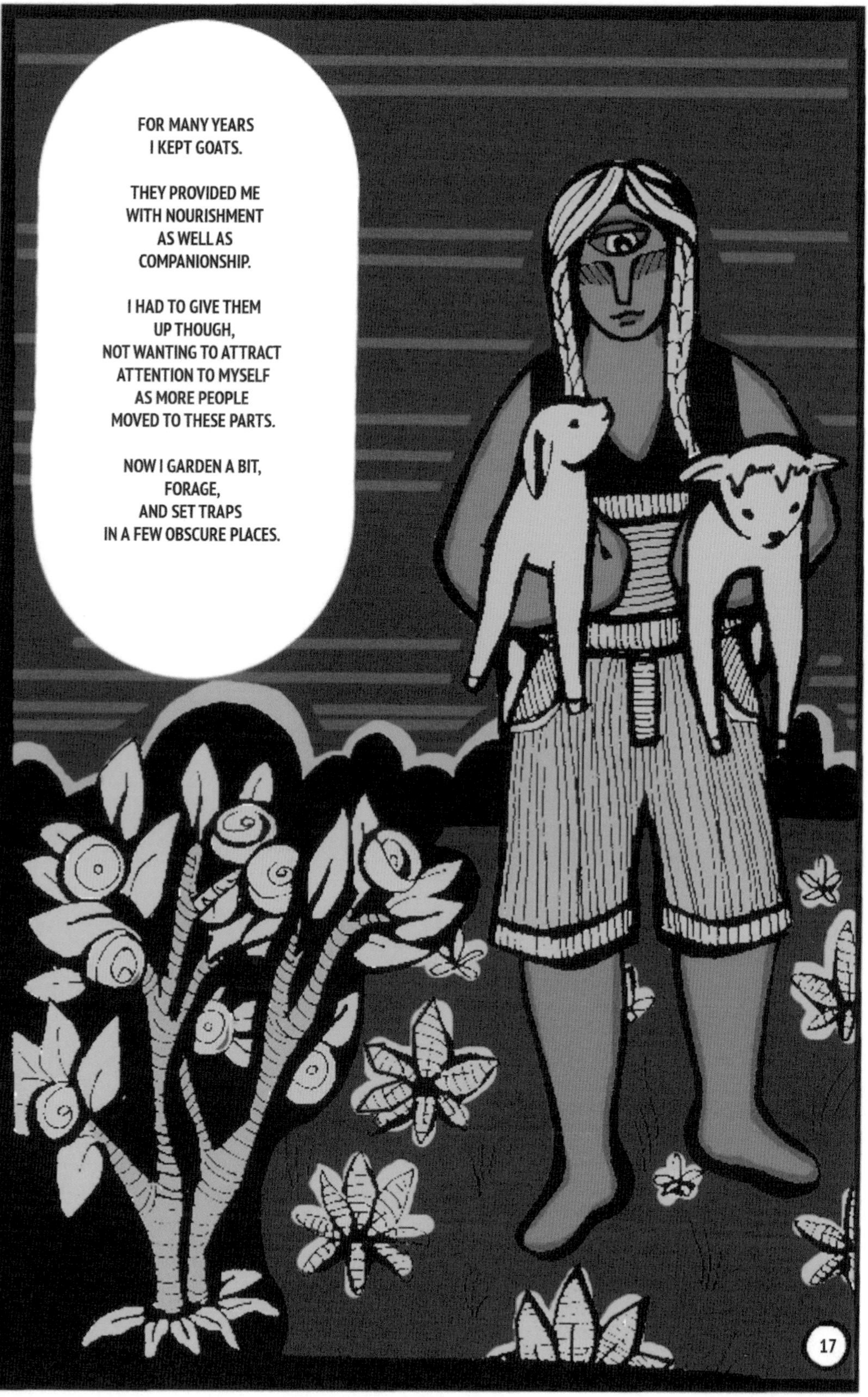
FOR MANY YEARS
I KEPT GOATS.
THEY PROVIDED ME
WITH NOURISHMENT
AS WELL AS
COMPANIONSHIP.
I HAD TO GIVE THEM
UP THOUGH,
NOT WANTING TO ATTRACT
ATTENTION TO MYSELF
AS MORE PEOPLE
MOVED TO THESE PARTS.
NOW I GARDEN A BIT,
FORAGE,
AND SET TRAPS
IN A FEW OBSCURE PLACES.

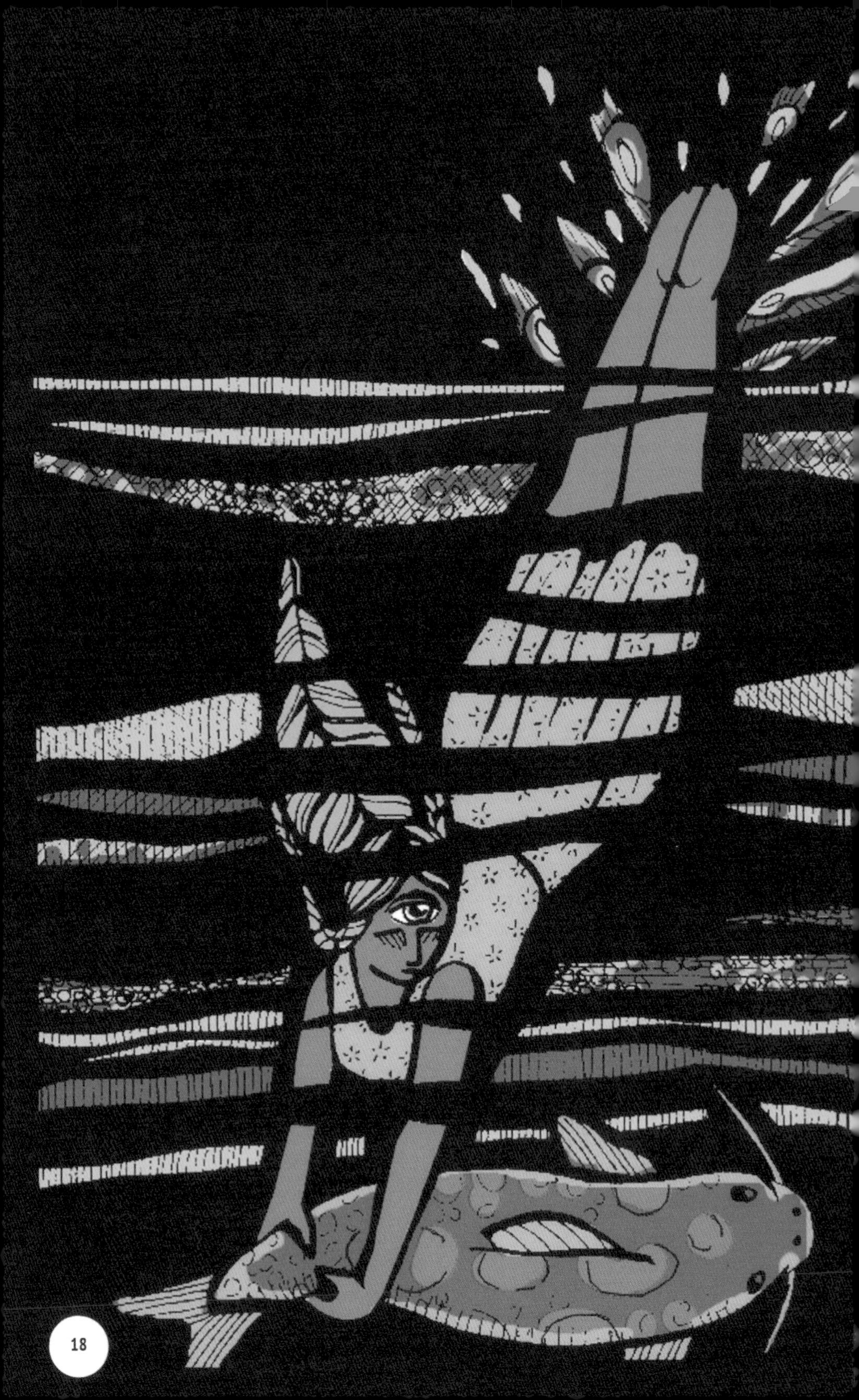

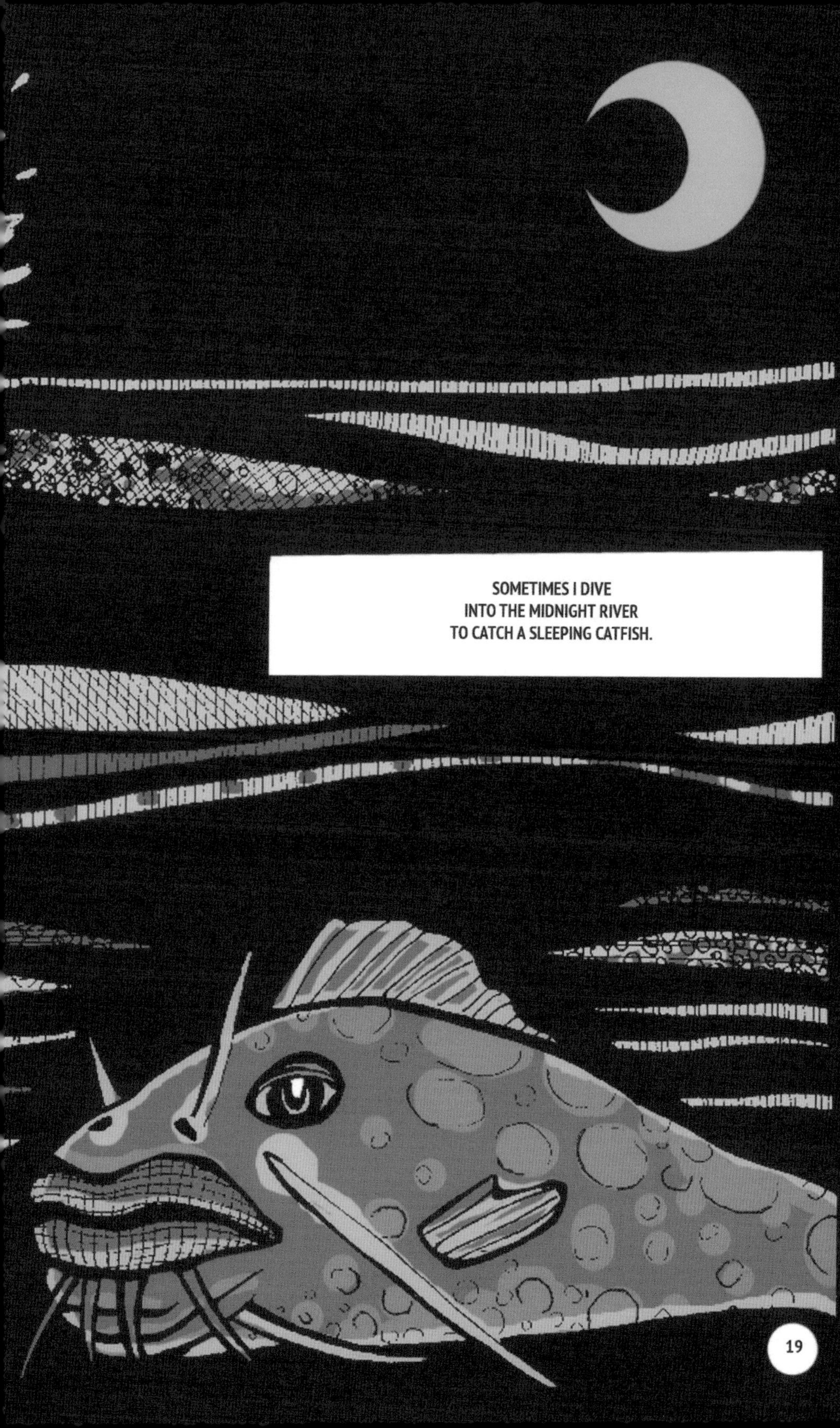
SOMETIMES I DIVE
INTO THE MIDNIGHT RIVER
TO CATCH A SLEEPING CATFISH.

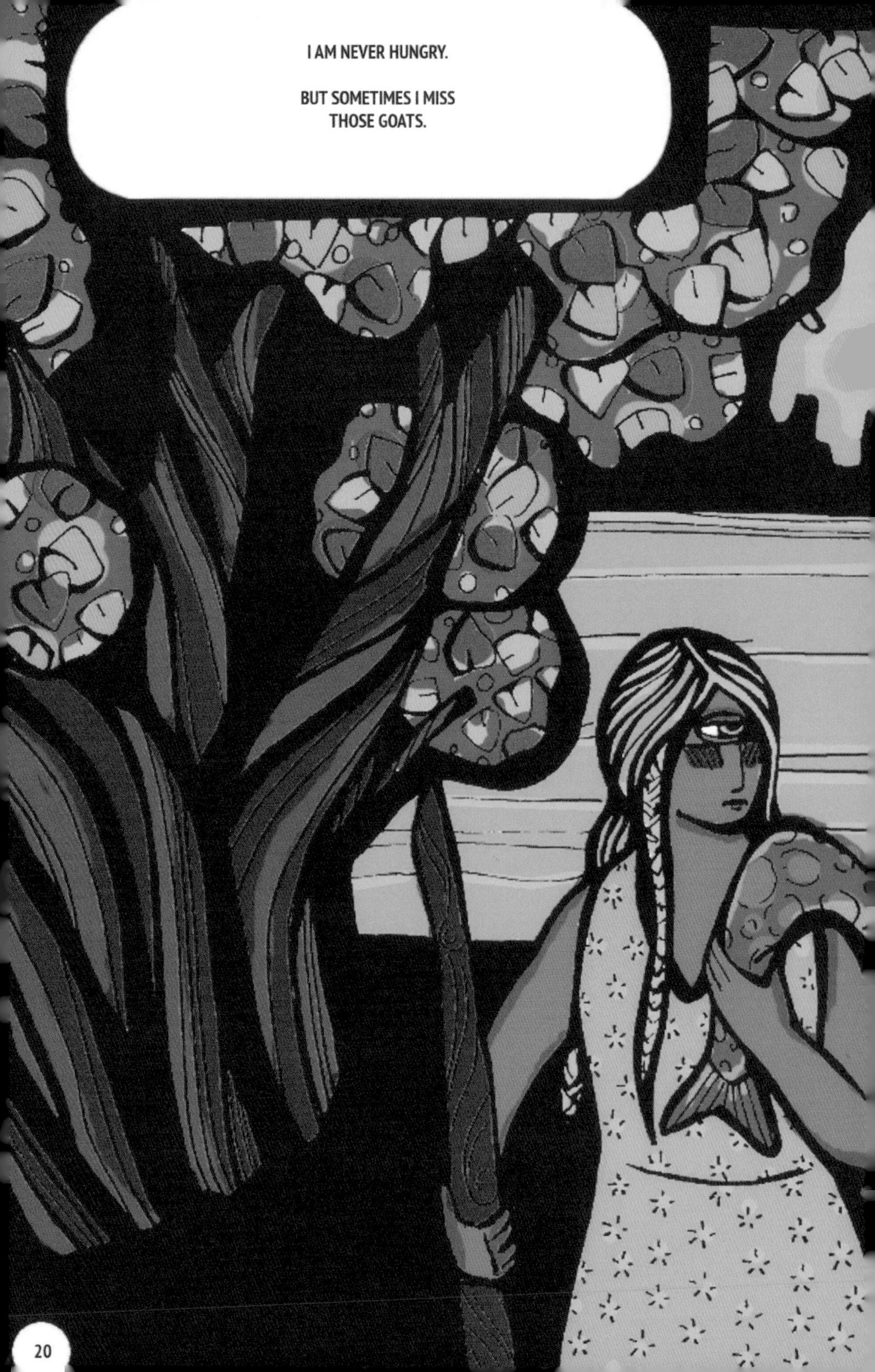
I AM NEVER HUNGRY.
BUT SOMETIMES I MISS THOSE GOATS.

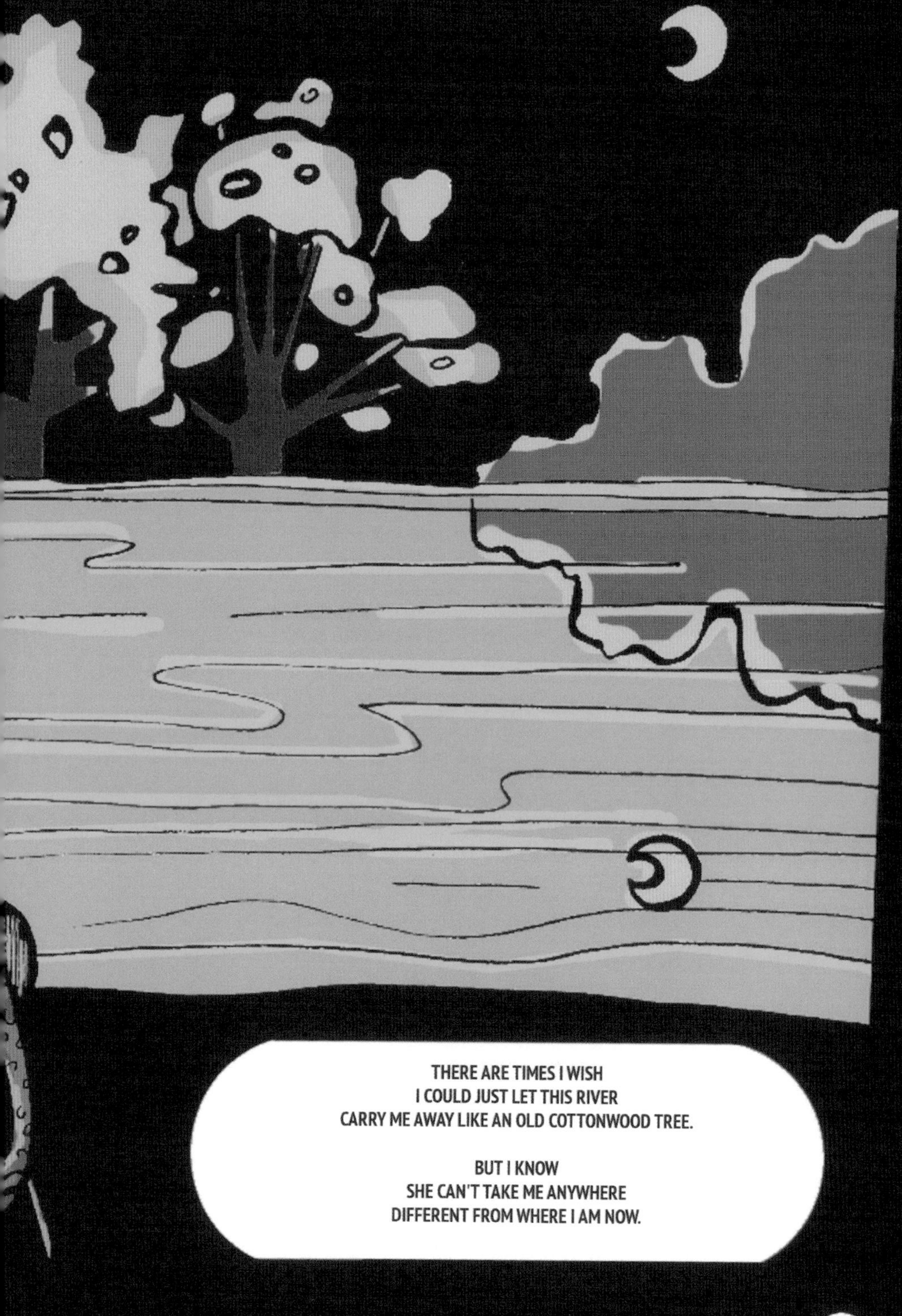
THERE ARE TIMES I WISH
I COULD JUST LET THIS RIVER
CARRY ME AWAY LIKE AN OLD COTTONWOOD TREE.
BUT I KNOW
SHE CAN'T TAKE ME ANYWHERE
DIFFERENT FROM WHERE I AM NOW.

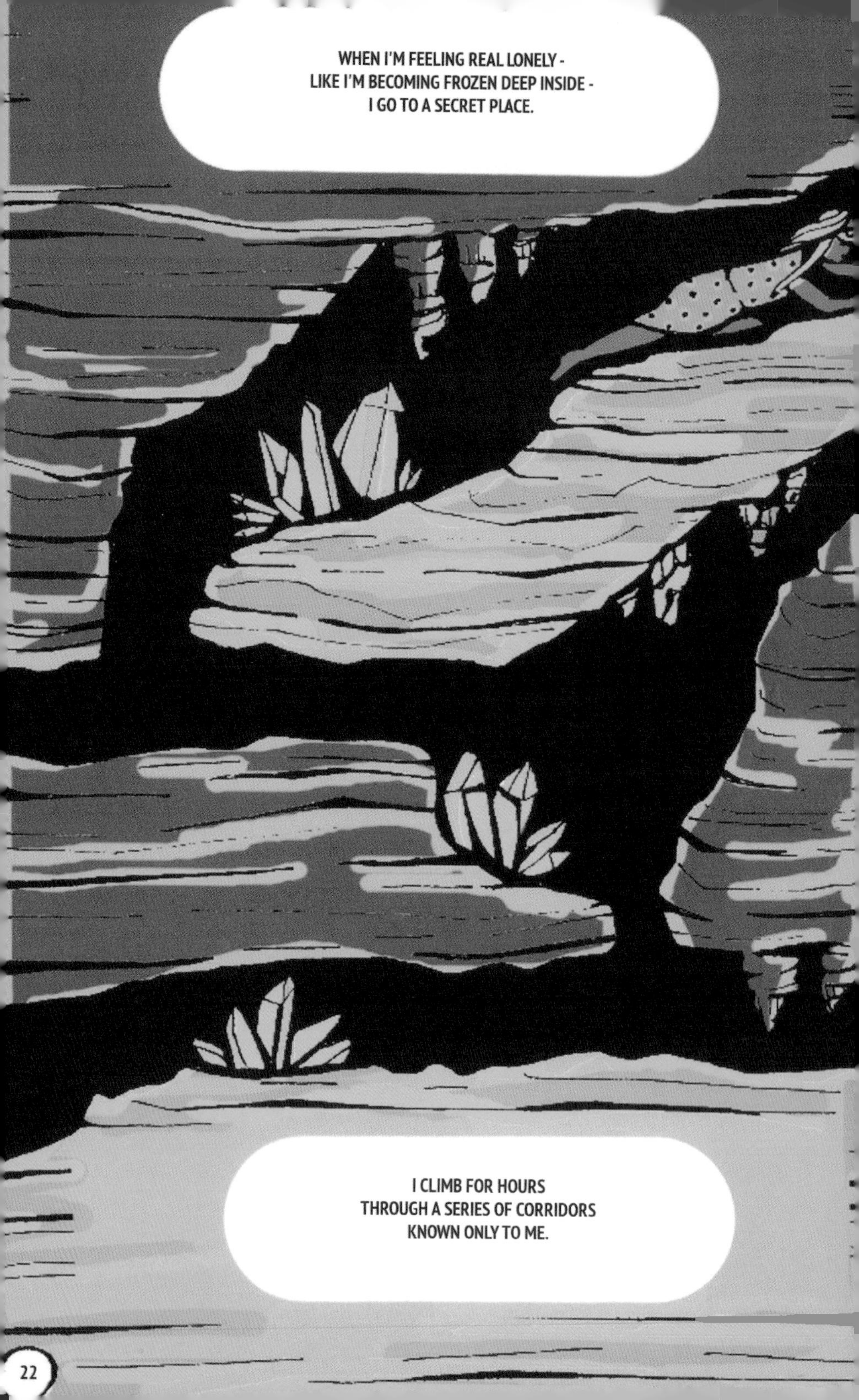
WHEN I'M FEELING REAL LONELY - LIKE I'M BECOMING FROZEN DEEP INSIDE - I GO TO A SECRET PLACE.
I CLIMB FOR HOURS THROUGH A SERIES OF CORRIDORS KNOWN ONLY TO ME.

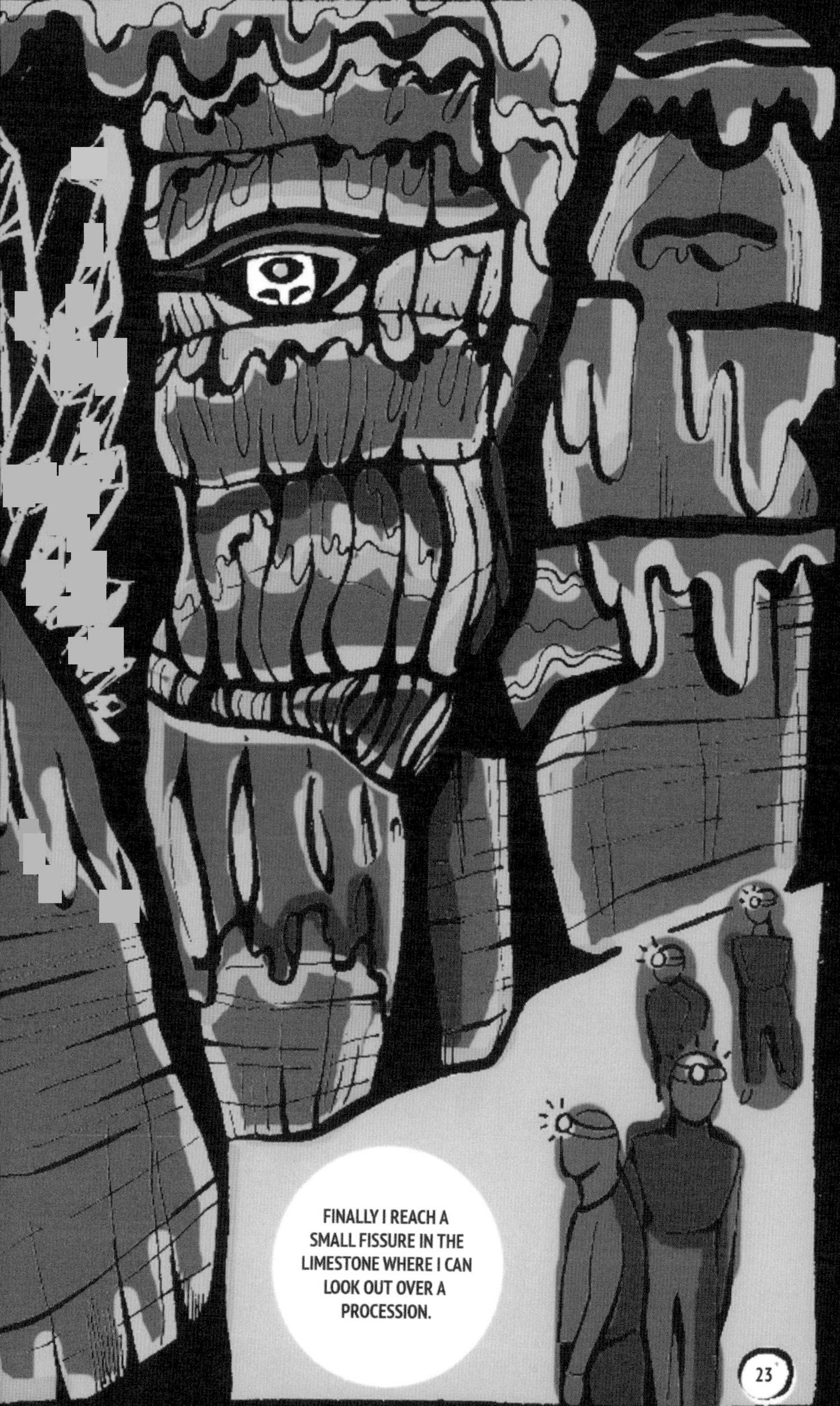
FINALLY I REACH A SMALL FISSURE IN THE LIMESTONE WHERE I CAN LOOK OUT OVER A PROCESSION.

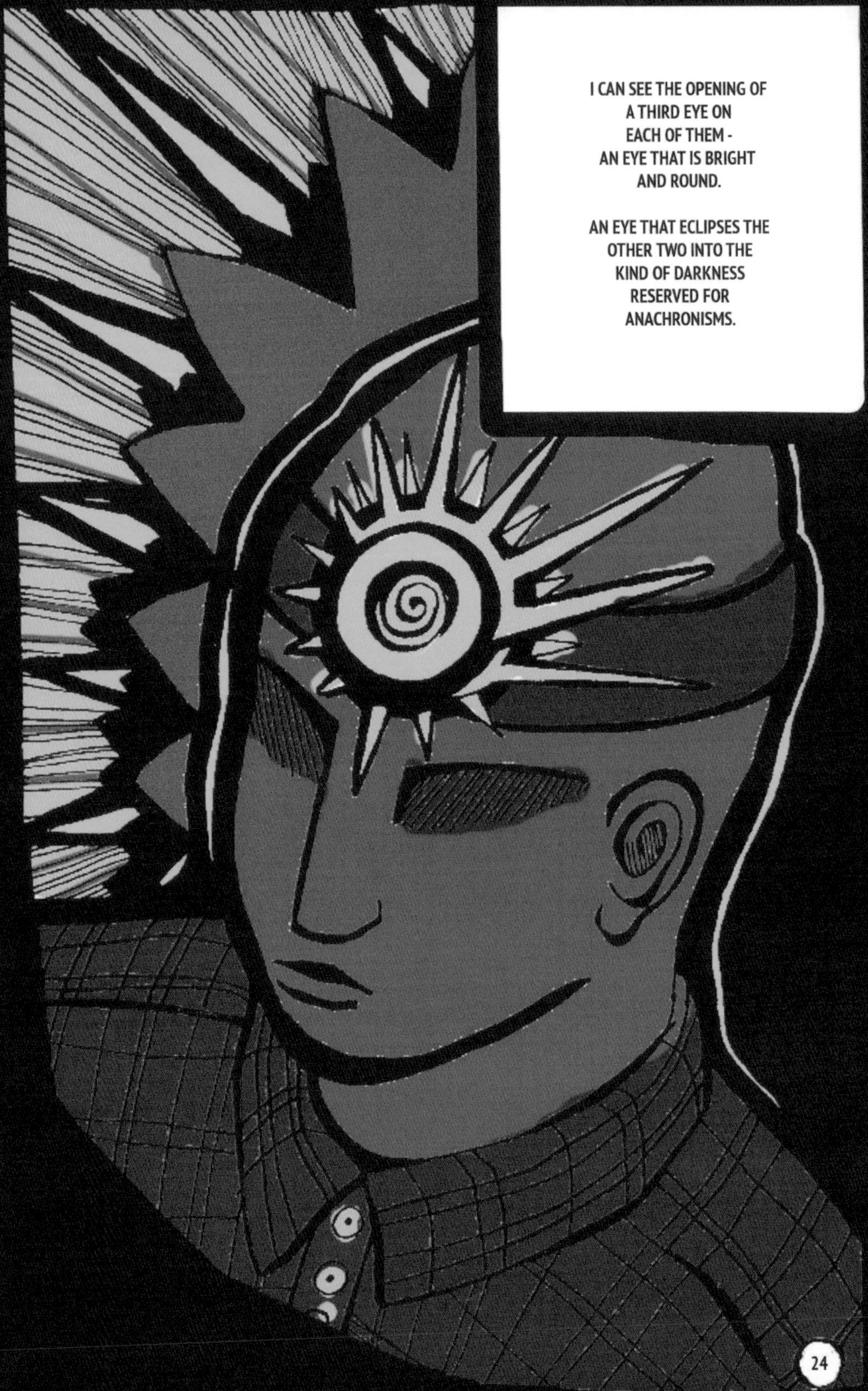
I CAN SEE THE OPENING OF
A THIRD EYE ON
EACH OF THEM -
AN EYE THAT IS BRIGHT
AND ROUND.

AN EYE THAT ECLIPSES THE
OTHER TWO INTO THE
KIND OF DARKNESS
RESERVED FOR
ANACHRONISMS.

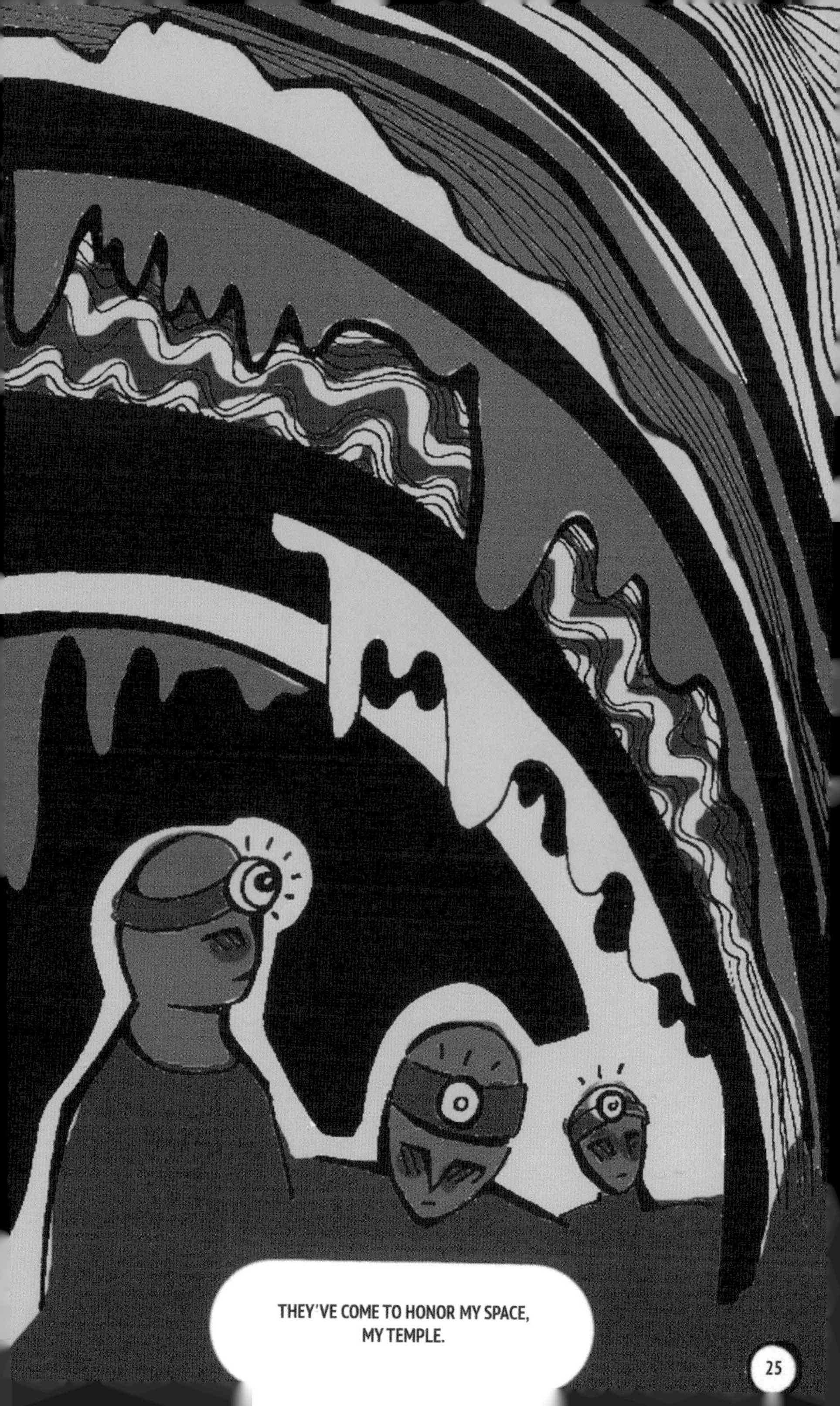
THEY'VE COME TO HONOR MY SPACE, MY TEMPLE.

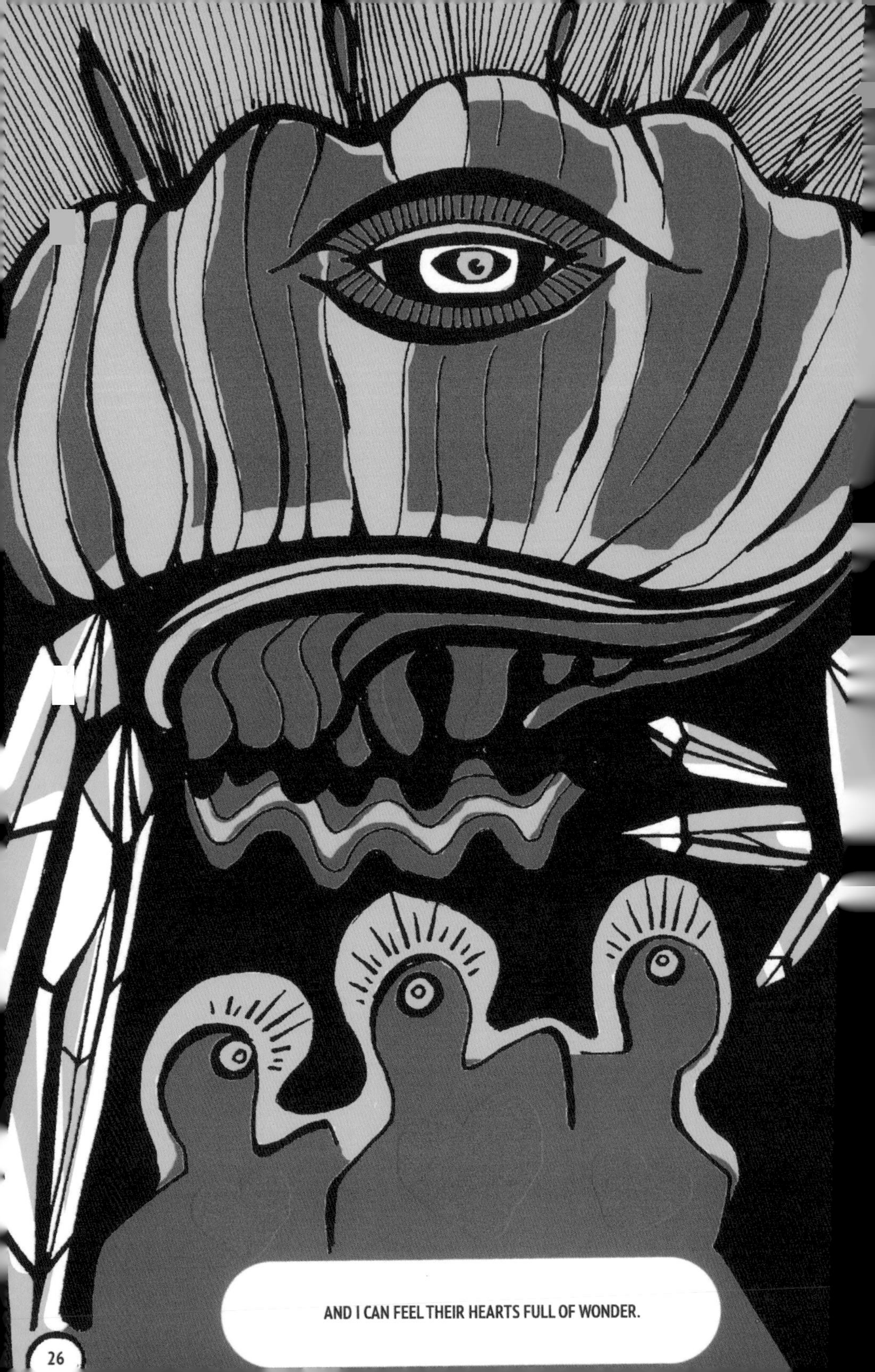
AND I CAN FEEL THEIR HEARTS FULL OF WONDER.

Sarah Goodnow Riley-Land has lived in Columbia, Missouri
for 20 years and counting. She makes art and other handmade objects
inspired by magical beings and the Missouri River. She works in a
converted studio space (read: spare bedroom) in her home
under the name Midnight River.

Find out more or contact the author at

midnightriver.design

Follow Midnight River on Instagram
@midnight_river

Made in the USA
Lexington, KY
21 September 2016